THE COMIC STRIP BOOK

PETER FOSTER

SCHOLASTIC INC.
New York Toronto London Auckland Sydney

To my father, Harry, who always took a great interest in my childish scribbles.

A special thanks to James L Kemsley, who suggested and encouraged the making of this book.

Acknowledgments
I wish to thank James H Kemsley, writer of the Sunday strip, 'Ballantyne', and Derrick Warren, writer of 'Shannon', for samples from both in this book.

ISBN 0-590-48533-4

12 11 10 9 8 7 6 5 4 3 2 1   4 5 6 7 8 9/9

Printed in the U.S.A.   08

First Scholastic printing, September 1994

CONTENTS

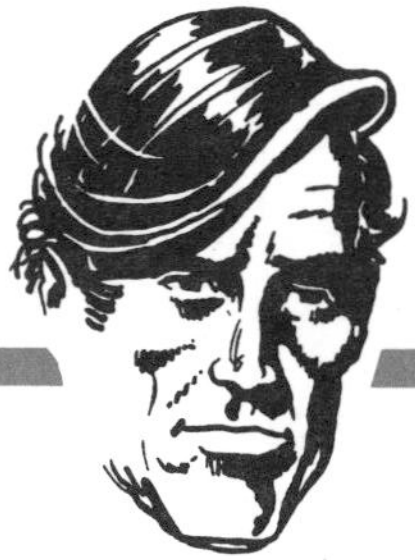

STORY STRIPS

Have you ever tried your hand at writing and drawing story strips? It can be hard work, but it's also a lot of fun and your finished product gives you great satisfaction!

Here is a sequence drawn by a young friend of mine, Lee Gladman. He was only 15 when he drew it.

The story is an interesting one. A police lecturer, wanting to inject some life into a seminar, fakes an attempted assassination of the chief of police to teach the anti-terrorist squad the dos and don'ts of handling an unexpected attack.

Pages 3 and 4 of 'Assassin', which show a fine grasp of moving from stillness to action.

YOUR CHOICE OF CHARACTER IS UNLIMITED,
but design a character who is easy to reproduce each time.

THUNDERMAN

Names are also fun to think up, but don't be too serious.

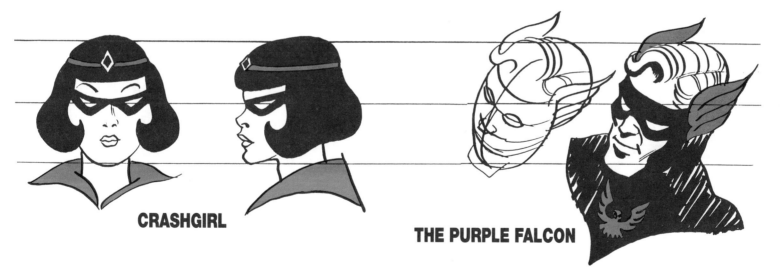

CRASHGIRL

THE PURPLE FALCON

You might find names in all sorts of places. Try science for names like Atom and Neutron or the animal world for Taipan and Tiger. Mythology gives you Red Zeus and insect names could include Wasp or Red Back. The choice is yours.

Note: Background characters are fun to create and they usually appear only once. Watch for those introducing some of these pages.

YOU COULD EVEN CHOOSE YOUR HERO OR HEROINE from an everyday situation.

DR DENISE
city casualty

LIEUTENANT STANTON
federal police

CINDY the maid
undercover agent

CHARLIE ROACH
stockman on a cattle station

SANDRA SILVERS
TV actress

But it's always best to choose a subject that you know something about. Your special interests should give you a clue. Sports stories work well.

STORY AND SCRIPT

A synopsis is an overall view of a story and should be clearly mapped out first.

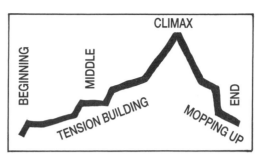

1 A story has a beginning (who and what's involved).

2 A middle (the ongoing events and the conflicts).

3 A climax (the high point of the excitement).

4 And an end (the solution to the problem and the 'mopping up').

Happy endings are best in a comic strip.

You might be a good artist but not great at thinking up stories. Why not involve a friend who is good at storytelling and writing? This is called collaboration.

'The Eagle' was a superhero invented by Carl Lyon, an Australian artist from the 1940s. It is drawn here by Peter Foster.

BEGINNING

MIDDLE

CLIMAX

END But not the last frame. There's a little mopping up to do.

WRITE each separate event on a different card (or use your word processor).

BEGINNING	MIDDLE	END
Thunderman (T) is called in to rescue some hostages in a city bank which is being robbed....	(T) enters bank and confronts the robbers.....	(T) overcomes the robbers and rescues the hostages!

This is really dull stuff at the moment. What we need to do is to develop the MIDDLE with a lot more events and build the tension to a CLIMAX.

Each event should cause an effect. Each action should have a counteraction.

The best way is to ask yourself lots of questions.

How does THUNDERMAN get into the bank?

Do the robbers know he is there?

Do they overcome him at first?

Do they hold the upper hand?

How many are there? (not too many or it will be too hard to draw them)

What superpowers does THUNDERMAN have?

Does he use these powers to win the conflict?

Does the chief robber escape?

Is there a chase? (Perhaps a car crash?)

All the answers to these questions are your story!

YOUR STORY at this stage, with the addition of more cards, might read like this!

BEGINNING

Police chief calls in Thunderman (T) to rescue hostages from bank.

(T) can fly through solid walls. Bullets can pass through him, without hurting. (T) enters bank through back wall.

MIDDLE

Robbers see (T) and threaten to machine-gun the girl teller and the manager. (T) plays for time.

Chief robber tells sidekick to tie up (T) to a chair. (T) pretends to be tied up but he can pass through ropes too.

Police chief outside bank is in contact with robber chief by phone. Robbers demand a helicopter for escape!

(T) uses a distraction to disappear into a wall. Police agree to chopper for crooks escape. They think (T) must have failed.

CLIMAX

(T)'s arms come out of a wall to disable and disarm the 2nd robber. Robber chief panics !!!

Bank manager and girl run into vault and pull the door closed. They are locked in and can't get out!

Robber chief runs into lift to go to the roof where chopper will land....

(T) passes into vault to get instructions to open vault. The hostages are now safe.

(T) passes through all floors and into back of chopper. The robber chief has the pilot covered with machine gun....

END

(T) disarms robber chief who is totally amazed... so is the chopper pilot.
Final clean up as crooks are given to police. SMILES!! SMILES!

WHA...?

?!

BANG!

BUT THIS IS *MY* STORY! *YOU* CAN THINK UP A *BETTER* ONE!

Number your cards and insert more cards as necessary.

ROUGHS: A very quick design of your page in a small version helps you to iron out potential problems.

Write your BOXES and BALLOONS on your ROUGHS.
Basically, try to 'rough out' the whole story.

POLICE CHIEF CRANSTON SEEKS THE AID OF THUNDERMAN!

HOSTAGES ARE BEING HELD AT THE BANK!

THAT'S ALWAYS THE HARDEST THING TO COPE WITH!!

ANYTHING MIGHT HAPPEN!

BE CAREFUL THUNDERMAN! ONE OF THE GIRLS IS MY NIECE!

DON'T WORRY, CHIEF! I'LL RESCUE HER INTACT!

GOOD LUCK!

THUNDERMAN HAS THE POWER TO WALK AND FLY THROUGH WALLS AND OTHER SOLID MATERIAL AS HE WILLS.

THIS SURE SAVES A LOT OF TIME!

BOX → POLICE CHIEF CRANSTON

DIALOGUE BALLOON → HOSTAGES ARE BEING HELD AT THE BANK, THUNDERMAN!

THINK BALLOON → THAT'S ALWAYS THE HARDEST THING TO COPE WITH!

SOUND EFFECT → RING-RING!

10

LAYOUT AND PENCILLING:

Now, assemble all the usual cartoonists' tools: paper, HB pencil, rule, set square, compass and eraser, and begin to draw up your comic book pages. Do what most professionals do and draw your comics at least 1½ times the size needed for printing.

You start with a SPLASH page (see credits page). The SPLASH page is usually a right-hand page with an uneven page number. (Did you know that all right-handed pages in a book have uneven page numbers and all left-handed pages have even numbers?)

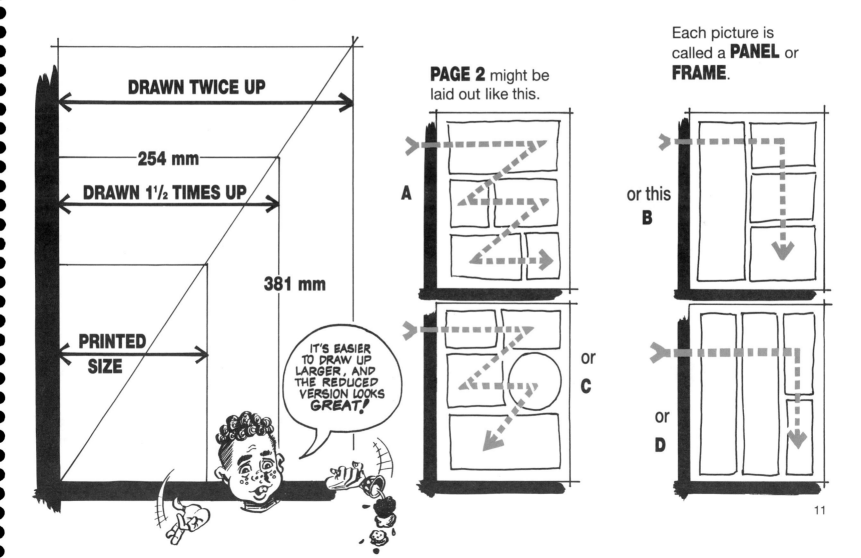

DRAWN TWICE UP

254 mm

DRAWN 1½ TIMES UP

381 mm

PRINTED SIZE

IT'S EASIER TO DRAW UP LARGER, AND THE REDUCED VERSION LOOKS GREAT!

PAGE 2 might be laid out like this.

A

or C

Each picture is called a **PANEL** or **FRAME**.

or this B

or D

BUT AVOID THIS ONE

because the reader will want to go from FRAME 1 to FRAME 4. You could put in arrows to show the reader which frame to read next, but it won't look as good.

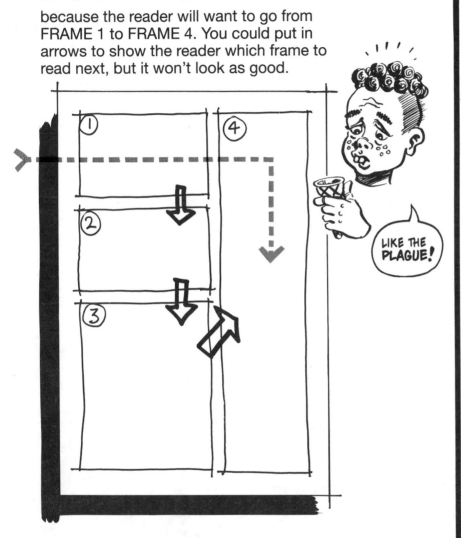

LIKE THE PLAGUE!

Here is an example of LAYOUT B from page 11. This section could be considered as ONE of the CLIMAXES in the story.

This example shows three frames within another frame. Any number of frames could be used within reason.

LETTERING: Lettering which is hard-to-read will simply put your reader off!

Use only a small number of words each time and try to stick to just one point in each balloon. Traditionally, CAPITAL LETTERS are used in both boxes and balloons.

Note: Leave plenty of space between the lettering and the balloon edge.

Note: Use lightly pencilled guidelines for the top and bottom of each line of lettering. The space between the lines of lettering should be half the letter height.

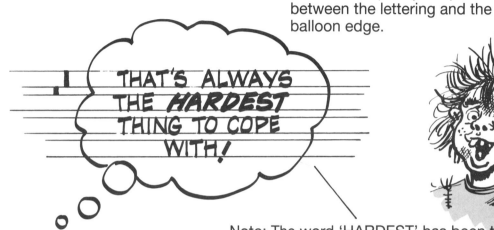

THAT'S ALWAYS THE *HARDEST* THING TO COPE WITH!

BE NEAT!

Note: Letters are formed with THIN VERTICALS and THICK TILTED HORIZONTALS.

Note: The word 'HARDEST' has been treated with BOLD letters and ITALICS (that's the term used for letters which lean at a racy angle).

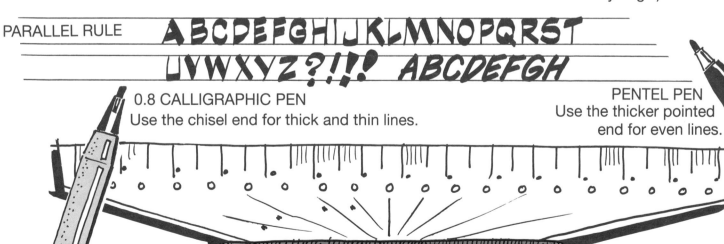

PARALLEL RULE ABCDEFGHIJKLMNOPQRST UVWXYZ?!!! *ABCDEFGH*

0.8 CALLIGRAPHIC PEN
Use the chisel end for thick and thin lines.

PENTEL PEN
Use the thicker pointed end for even lines.

ROLLER RULER

THE AMOUNT OF LETTERING in each frame
should be kept to a minimum. Too much, and you've lost your reader.

A PICTURE IS WORTH A THOUSAND WORDS!

Very bad!

THANK YOU FOR THE BIRTHDAY PRESENT, MYRA! IT'S QUITE INTERESTING! ACTUALLY, THE WORD "ENIGMATIC" COMES TO MIND. FOR INSTANCE: WHY IS THERE ONLY **ONE**? AND WHAT CAN I INFER FROM ITS ANTIQUITY? IS THERE SOME HIDDEN SYMBOLISM IN THE THIN DRY CAKING OF **MUD**? OR DOES THAT CAKING COME FROM AN EVEN *MORE* DISTURBING SOURCE?

A-HEM!

AND THE WRAPPING PAPER *ITSELF* SPEAKS ***VOLUMES!*** A LOT OF THOUGHT HAS GONE INTO IT, MYRA.

ACTUALLY, MY BIRTHDAY WAS THREE WEEKS AGO... BUT... NO PROBS!

Not too good!

HELLO, MYRA? I'M JUST RINGING TO SAY HOW THOUGHTFUL OF YOU TO SEND ME A PRESENT TO COMMEMORATE MY BIRTHDAY! I MUST SAY IT'S VERY TOUCHING! THE SYMBOLISM, *HOWEVER*, I FIND VERY ELUSIVE! HELLO ...

ARE YOU THERE, MYRA?

... MYRA?

Ah! Much better!

THANKS FOR THE BIRTHDAY PRESENT, MYRA! DOES THIS MEAN OUR RELATIONSHIP IS LIKE...

OVER?

TO BIRD BRAIN

PROPORTIONS AND ANATOMY of the human figure need to be studied all the time. You might as well start NOW!

Basic proportions can be used for male and female figures. As you learn and observe more, you can work out the differences yourself.

The thick black line is the AXIS (the plural of axis is axes). Notice that when it curves, the figure seems to have more life.

THIS is how a pencilled page might look.

The pencilled pages are called 'the pencils'. Sometimes one artist will do the pencils and a different artist will do 'the inks'. In such a case, the pencils need to be very accurate. But if you do both pencils and inks, especially when you become experienced, the pencils can be much rougher.

SPEED LINES only work when the drawing already has ACTION. Note the ANGLE of the AXES.

'AXES' IS PRONOUNCED AXEES!

All the axes of the parts of the body shown here are on the vertical and horizontal. Not much ACTION here despite SPEED LINES.

Most of the axes in this drawing are off the vertical and horizontal. All of these angles add 'dynamism' to the figure. Now the SPEED LINES are much more effective.

More on the importance of 'direction of the axes' is found on pages 53–55.

FORESHORTENING (where parts of the body are coming towards you) can be enhanced by strong tonal differences.

EXPRESSION IN FACES helps to tell a story with feeling. POSTURE helps to create a mood.

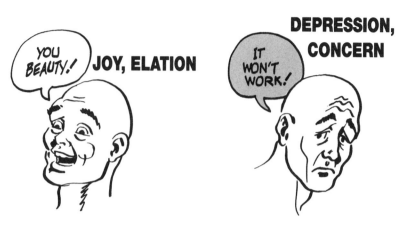

JOY, ELATION

DEPRESSION, CONCERN

ANGER

MIRTH

Note the shape, angle and distance between the eyes and eyebrows in each case.

Study the different AXES of the figures. To help you achieve the right expression in a drawing, do some acting and clowning in front of a mirror.

HUMAN EMOTION

has to be part of a story so that the reader *feels* the same way as the hero, heroine or other characters.

JUBILATION

SMUGNESS

DERISION

ANGRY DETERMINATION

ADMIRATION and APPREHENSION

A TRY-ON

OOPS!

SNOBBERY

RELIEF AFTER FEAR

FRUSTRATION AND SELF-RIGHTEOUSNESS (Note: axes)

**FEMININE CAJOLEMENT
AND RELUCTANT
ACCEPTANCE**

ANGRY CONFRONTATION AND SHOCK

**EXCUSES, EXCUSES AND
TEARFUL DISAPPOINTMENT**

SOME STORIES give rise to many more subtle
variations in emotional expression, while others tend
to concentrate on physical action. Both are fun to draw.

INKING:

Gather together the tools and materials needed for inking. If you intend using a small brush for inking lines, it should be one of excellent quality. It is much cheaper to use a pen or a marker.

Light blue pencil lines do not photograph, so erasing your rough lines is unnecessary. But they will show up on a photocopy.

Ordinary black pencil lines must be erased after inking. Sometimes the ink is thinned down by erasing and has to be touched up again.

But why is THUNDERMAN feeling so weak in the legs?

LINES should be varied in thickness to help give THREE-DIMENSIONAL SOLIDITY and also 'flare' to your style.

THUNDERMAN feels weak in the legs because the lines used to draw them are 'weak'.

Vary the pressure on the nib.

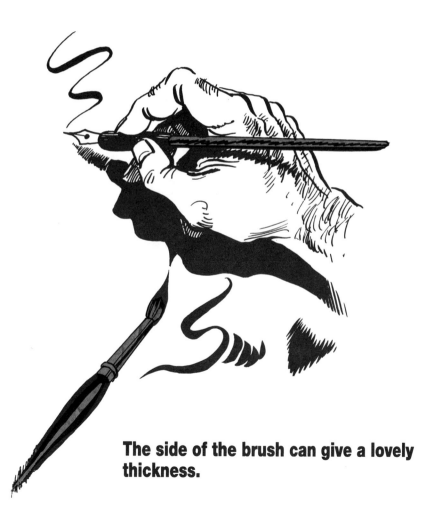

The side of the brush can give a lovely thickness.

Don't be afraid to have a full black shadow under limbs, but the drawing of it must be done carefully.

MISTAKES IN INK may be whited out with GRAPHIC WHITE, PROCESS WHITE, CHINESE WHITE or, better still, PLAKA. LIQUID PAPER is too hard to draw back over, so should be avoided.

SO-CALLED INK RUBBER . . .

NEVER try to erase ink. It will **TOTAL** your drawing. Sometimes it's best to start all over again . . .

. . . BUT NOT THE WHOLE PAGE.

Just *that* frame or part of it!

Patch it in or paste it down over the wreckage.
When printed or photocopied you can't tell the difference

. . . and talking about PHOTOCOPIES . . .

PHOTOCOPIES (good clean black ones) can be used in many ways.

1 A good drawing may be too large or small, reduce or enlarge to suit, then paste down on your strip.

2 You may need to repeat a drawing in a story, such as a location which crops up a lot.

3 You can cut out figures from previous drawings and position or angle them differently.

4 You may polarise the many tones of a photograph to a black-and-white drawing by retouching and recopying—say, for complicated subjects. Many professionals do! Why shouldn't you?

HATCHING is a way of rendering flat areas of grey.

HATCHING   CROSSHATCHING   3 OR 4 WAYS   TEXTURES OF VARIOUS VALUES

This now gives you three or more tonal values to make your pictures more interesting;
black, white and grey. Little or no hatching should be used if you are colouring-in your art.

No outline has been used for the moon or the highlighted side of the figures. The hatching simply stops, to give the necessary contour. This 'softness' on the edge helps to suggest the moonlit atmosphere.

CAMERA ANGLES: LONG SHOTS, MEDIUM SHOTS and CLOSE-UPS

We can liken drawing a story strip to making a film or a video. Imagine you are using a camera from different distances and angles.

MEDIUM SHOT

LONG SHOT ON AN ANGLE

CLOSE-UP

Varying the choice of visual approach from panel to panel is stimulating for the reader.

HIGH AND LOW EYE LEVELS can also be used to good effect, but it makes the drawing harder.

HIGH EYE LEVEL gives the reader a bird's-eye view.

LOW EYE LEVEL gives the reader a worm's-eye view.

We will look at this concept in further detail again in the pages on 'perspective', starting on page 38.

29

PANEL SHAPES can also be changed . . . perhaps to heighten an emotional effect.

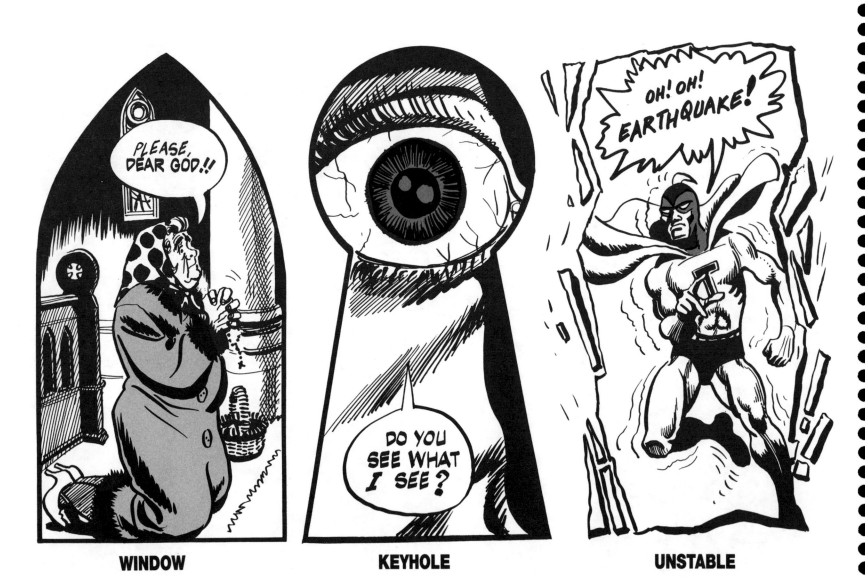

WINDOW

KEYHOLE

UNSTABLE

NEWSPAPER STRIPS: Daily and weekender strips need their own special approach to the story.

This daily shows how the last frame leaves the reader with a desire to catch tomorrow's strip to see what happens.

This is called a CLIFF-HANGER.

These two strips are from an unpublished daily called 'Shannon' by Derrick Warren and Peter Foster.

Here's another daily.

CLIFF-HANGERS should also occur in the last frame of a Sunday strip.

This strip moves from stillness to fast action. Frame 1 is still, but full of menace. Frame 2 shows the menace from another angle. Frame 3 starts the action. Frame 4 speeds up the action. The insert gives a close-up of why the drunken Scully loses his balance and frame 5 shows his total loss of control over his extremely dangerous situation.

This is a double CLIFF-HANGER! What is the warrior up to?

Will the croc eat Scully?

THE HUMAN EYE easily tires of too much detail, but is bored with not enough.

A LOT OF DETAIL

A 'LIMBO' BACKGROUND

SIMPLE BACKGROUND

Here the eye likes to wander around the picture, picking up the points of interest . . .

but now is happy to have a well-earned rest.

Back to a bit of work for the eye . . . but not too much. Just a suggestion of detail.

It's amazing how the imagination of the reader will fill in, when necessary. If the reader has occasion to recall the last frame without referring to it, they will remember a much fuller picture. This daily strip shows an example of a 'verbal' CLIFF-HANGER.

COSTUME AND CLOTHING
need to be reasonably convincing.

I'M FAIRLY EASY TO DRAW BECAUSE I'M REALLY ONLY THE *HUMAN FIGURE!*

BUT I'M *TOUGH* TO DRAW BECAUSE OF ALL THE *FOLDS* IN MY CLOTHES!

Sketch from life whenever you can. It's said that if you can draw the human figure, you can draw *anything*!

LIGHTLY DRAW MY FIGURE *FIRST...* THEN **ADD** MY CLOTHING!

FOLDS in clothing run between points of tension.

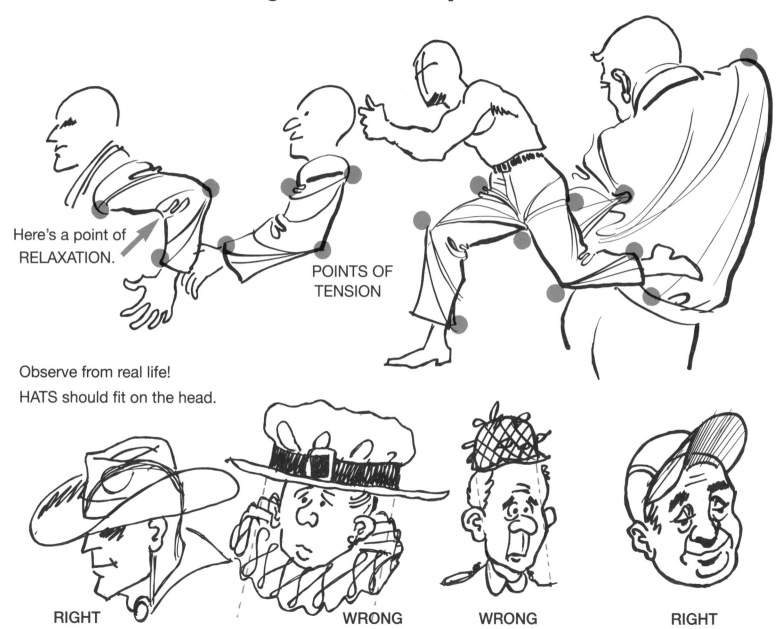

Here's a point of RELAXATION.

POINTS OF TENSION

Observe from real life!

HATS should fit on the head.

RIGHT   WRONG   WRONG   RIGHT

WALKING affects a girl's skirt. Any physical action creates effects in clothing.

FOLDS radiating from points of TENSION.

Twisting of the figure creates changing points of TENSION.

STAY COOL, MAN!

Note: The correct word for twisting of the figure is 'contrapposto'. Michelangelo and the later artists of the baroque period perfected this expression.

A costume in repose.

Points of TENSION are in the EAGLE's hands. Note how folds radiate from these points.

You decide where the points of TENSION are in these three illustrations.

Points of TENSION in BALLANTYNE's shirt are at the shoulders and under the armpits. Note how the shirt folds are relaxed just above the belt.

Period and specialist costumes require research.

PERSPECTIVE, EYE LEVEL AND VANISHING POINTS

PERSPECTIVE is very important
for capturing truth in space.

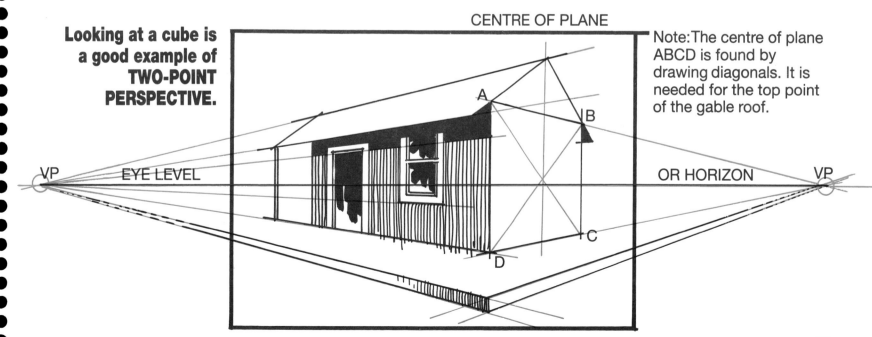

Looking down a street is a good example of **ONE-POINT PERSPECTIVE.**

EYE LEVEL

Note: VANISHING POINTS must always be on the EYE LEVEL.

VANISHING POINT (VP)

CENTRE OF PLANE

Looking at a cube is a good example of TWO-POINT PERSPECTIVE.

Note: The centre of plane ABCD is found by drawing diagonals. It is needed for the top point of the gable roof.

VP EYE LEVEL OR HORIZON VP

A
B
C
D

The HUMAN FIGURE has to be placed in perspective, too.

THIS FIGURE, E HAS BEEN PROJECTED FROM C. THEY ARE THE SAME DISTANCE AWAY.

EYE LEVEL

This is a LOW EYE LEVEL (see page 29) view of several figures in PERSPECTIVE. The entire figure, in real life, would be the same height but figures in the distance APPEAR smaller. Every figure's knees are on the EYE LEVEL. Waists could all go on the EYE LEVEL for a more normal view: heads are on the EYE LEVEL for a higher view.

EYE LEVEL (or HORIZON LINE) in this picture is just below the soldiers' belts. In this case, the PERSPECTIVE was just guessed.

With these three pictures from a detective story called 'Salmon', see if you can decide whether they are HIGH, LOW or MEDIUM EYE LEVEL and where their HORIZONS might be.

THE FOUNDATION IS INTO *EVERYTHING!*

THEY'D POLLUTE OUR *WATER,* IF IT WOULD MAKE A DOLLAR!

TUESDAY MORNING. 6·15...

BLUE DOLPHIN

THREE-POINT PERSPECTIVE

RIGHT VP

LEFT VP is on the HORIZON LINE, way off the page.

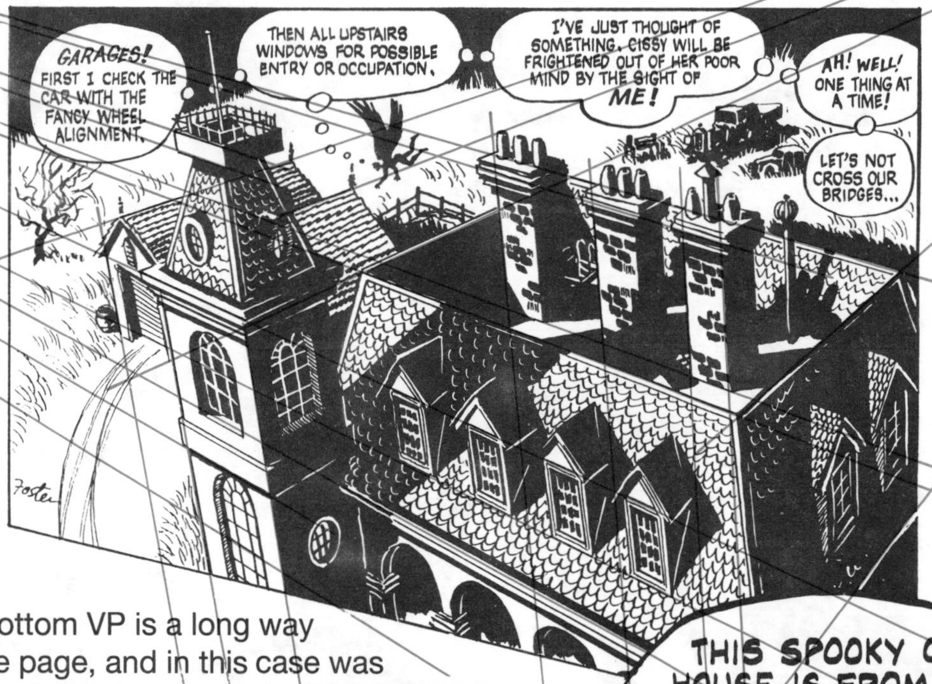
GARAGES! FIRST I CHECK THE CAR WITH THE FANCY WHEEL ALIGNMENT.
THEN ALL UPSTAIRS WINDOWS FOR POSSIBLE ENTRY OR OCCUPATION.
I'VE JUST THOUGHT OF SOMETHING. CISSY WILL BE FRIGHTENED OUT OF HER POOR MIND BY THE SIGHT OF ME!
AH! WELL! ONE THING AT A TIME!
LET'S NOT CROSS OUR BRIDGES...
Foster

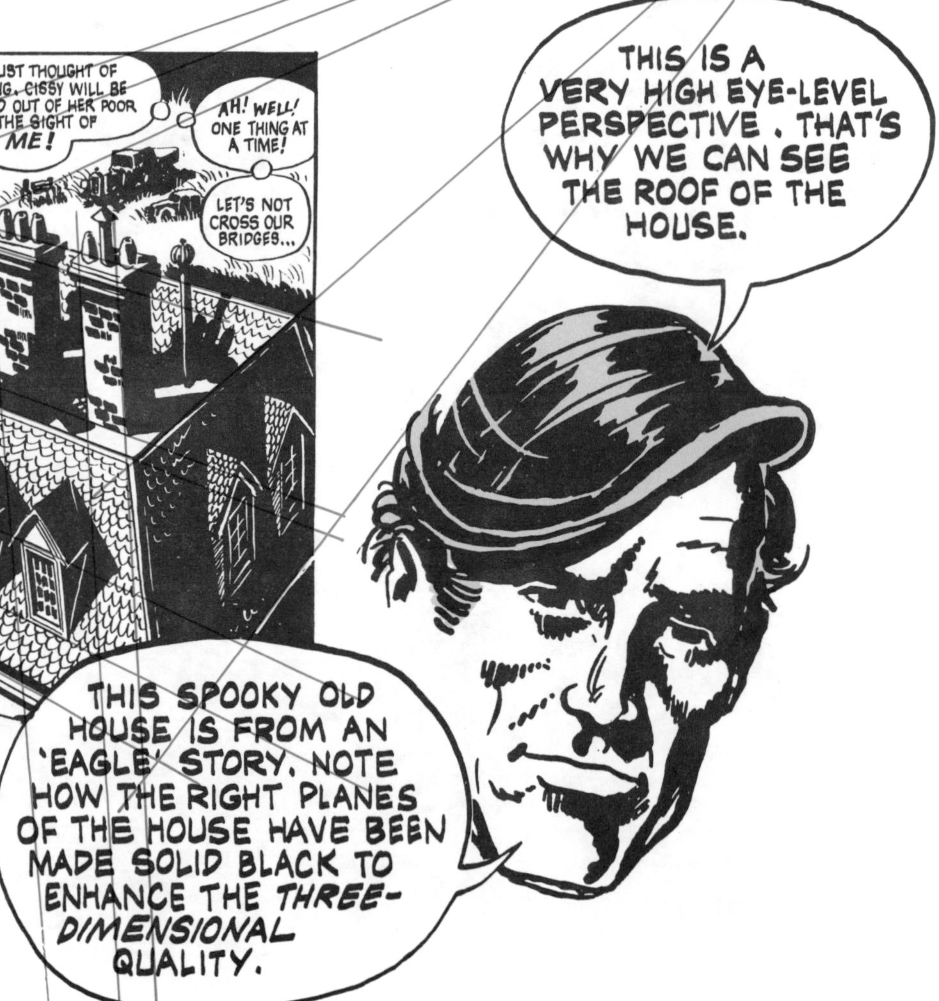
THIS IS A VERY HIGH EYE-LEVEL PERSPECTIVE. THAT'S WHY WE CAN SEE THE ROOF OF THE HOUSE.
THIS SPOOKY OLD HOUSE IS FROM AN 'EAGLE' STORY. NOTE HOW THE RIGHT PLANES OF THE HOUSE HAVE BEEN MADE SOLID BLACK TO ENHANCE THE THREE-DIMENSIONAL QUALITY.

The bottom VP is a long way off the page, and in this case was guessed. Total accuracy in THREE-POINT PERSPECTIVE requires a very large table top and a large area of paper, often just for a small picture. Where the VP is so far off the page, an estimated VP is sufficient. But you should have a good eye for it.

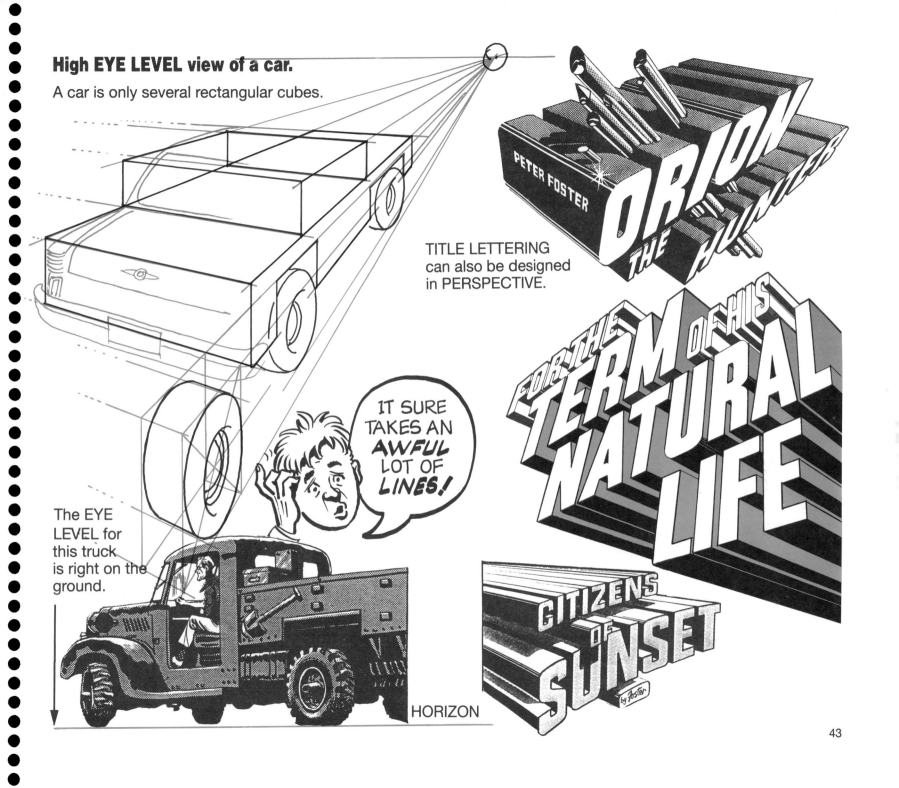

High EYE LEVEL view of a car.

A car is only several rectangular cubes.

TITLE LETTERING can also be designed in PERSPECTIVE.

The EYE LEVEL for this truck is right on the ground.

IT SURE TAKES AN *AWFUL* LOT OF *LINES!*

HORIZON

PETER FOSTER

ORION THE HUNTER

FOR THE TERM OF HIS NATURAL LIFE

CITIZENS OF SUNSET

by Foster

43

VISUAL REFERENCE MATERIAL is essential in the drawing of story strips. Even commonly used objects need to be looked at before inclusion in a picture.

THIS FISHING TRAWLER was designed from a composite of parts from other trawlers I had in my collection of magazine pictures.

THIS JAGUAR was traced from a photograph.

THIS JAPANESE ZERO was found in a book on World War II planes from my local library.

THIS TUDOR HOUSE was in my collection of magazine tear sheets filed under 'HOUSES'.

TRACING FROM PHOTOS

for the sake of realism is not cheating. Use your window or preferably a light-box. Never trace from other artists' work.

Don't trace directly from a magazine picture, because the printed matter on the back will show on the light-box, confusing the issue. Trace from a photocopy of it.

Note: A photocopied picture can be used the right way round or reversed left to right. You may need only part of it for your picture.

LIGHT-BOX

Leave unnecessary things out of your picture.

SILHOUETTING of complex objects is a good, fast and effective way of depicting them.

AN AUTHENTIC LOOK to settings and objects is essential if you want your story to be believed.

SPACE: As depicted by thrown shadows.

SHADOWS change direction when the planes they fall on change direction. The shadow in the above picture established that the figure is firmly supported by the ground plane and that he is standing close to a vertical plane, the wall.

LIGHTING, DRAMATIC OR SOFT, helps to
support the emotional idea at that point in the story.

BASIC ROUGH SHAPE

MECHANICAL TINTS are useful for grey areas.

A great variety of tones, printed onto a self-adhesive transparent film, can be purchased at an art shop.

LAID ON   **SURPLUS CUT AWAY WITH A SCALPEL.**

RUBBED ON

RUBBED ON TONES can be used on any surface within reason. Check with an art supplier for your special needs.

FRAMES can sometimes be left out altogether.

The great Will Eisner* says this can suggest vast open spaces such as in a desert, but sometimes it can be used to change a pattern across a strip. This gives visual relief and interest.

Sometimes it's fun to allow the subject to lean, run or fall out of the frame. These effects vary the pace and feel and stimulate interest in your reader.

*Eisner, Will. *Comics and Sequential Art*. Poorhouse Press.

PACE: Time can be speeded up or slowed down to good effect.

ACCELERATED MOTION

Action achieved in the least number of frames.

DECELERATED MOTION

Here, more frames are given to analyse the action for the reader. This slows down the action like 'slow motion' in a film. Very satisfying! Both ways are effective. Your choice will probably depend on how much space you have.

COMPOSITION is the placement of shapes in a frame

for their most appropriate accommodation, to put across the point of the story at that moment in the strongest terms.

Let's start with how ANGLES affect EMOTIONS.

HORIZONTAL

When horizontal lines dominate, a feeling of peace and quiet prevails. There is stillness . . . no motion.

VERTICAL

A dominance of vertical lines suggests strength, but still no motion.

NON-VERTICAL AND NON-HORIZONTAL

Various angles away from the horizontal and vertical create feelings of movement, disturbance, action and instability. If you are drawing an action scene, this is the way you must go.

RHYTHM IN CURVES

Whirlpool type 'rhythms' give plenty of movement.

ANALYSE the angles, horizontals and verticals in this picture.

Your chances of finding horizontals and verticals in this scene are remote. That's why there is so much action going on.

FOREGROUND, MIDDLE GROUND AND DISTANCE

Here are three talking heads. Very dull stuff!

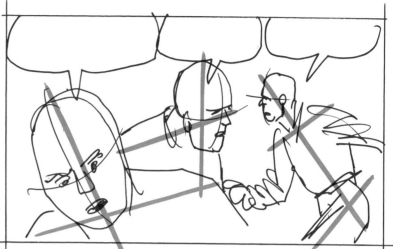

Here we have used various angles for their AXES, used FOREGROUND, MIDDLE GROUND and BACKGROUND, and each person is looking in a different direction. Much more interesting!

EH MISTER!

GROUPS OF FIGURES should make interesting shapes.

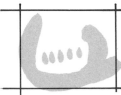

TREE AND WARRIOR form a circular frame around the distant figures.

THE SHAPE of this group makes us focus on a single character.

FOUR PLAYERS in the foreground form a strong triangle.

THIS GROUP creates an arrowhead, giving a forward motion.

SPECIAL ATMOSPHERICS and special lighting add to the emotional tension of a scene.

SNOW

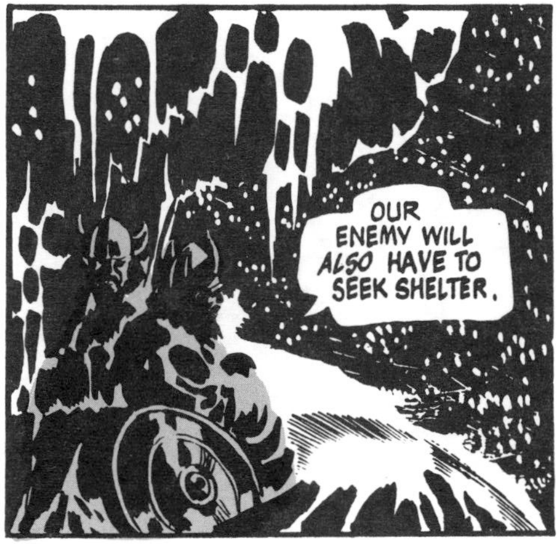
OUR ENEMY WILL ALSO HAVE TO SEEK SHELTER.

FIRE

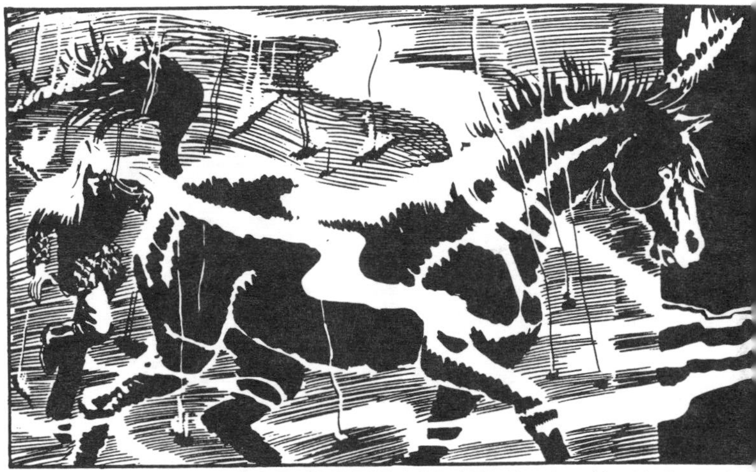

© D C THOMPSON & CO, LTD. Reprinted by kind permissi

RAIN

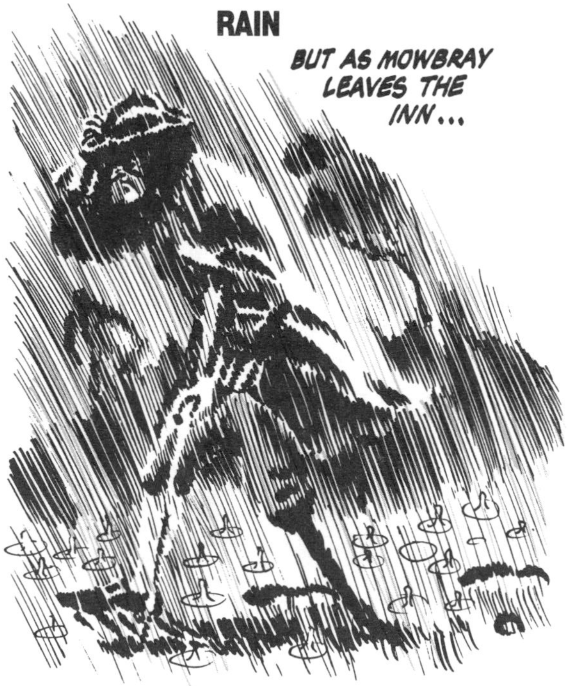
BUT AS MOWBRAY LEAVES THE INN...

FOG is suggested here by the horizontal lines which help to achieve an eerie stillness.

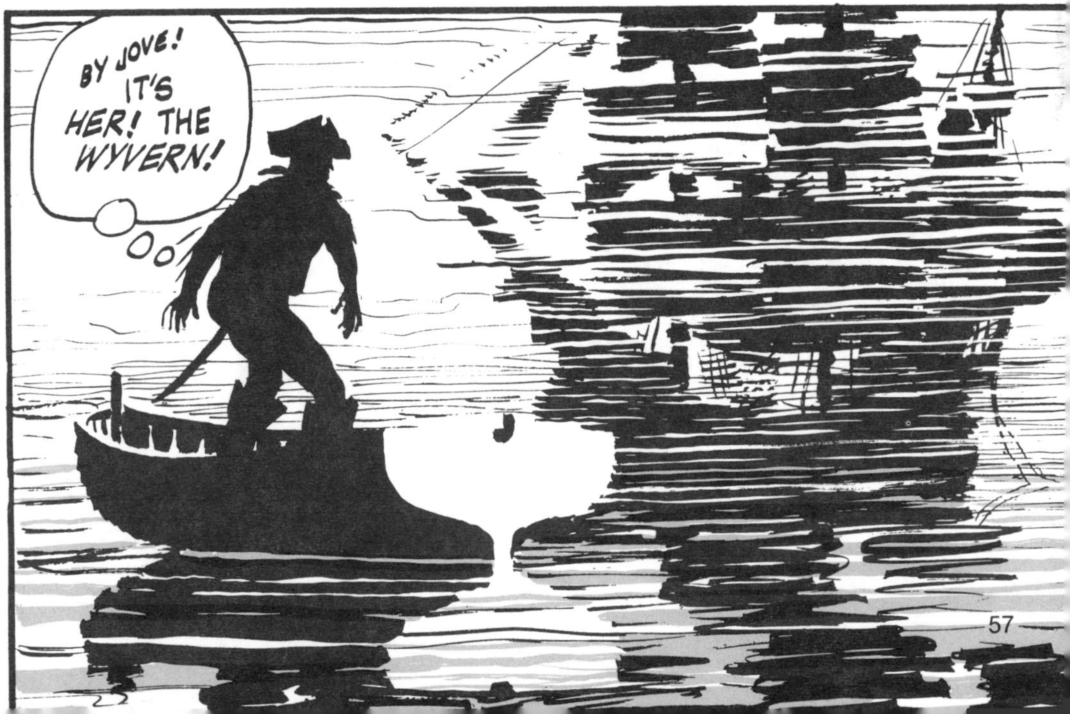
BY JOVE! IT'S HER! THE WYVERN!

MORE ATMOSPHERICS—fire, water, wind.

OIL, WATER, FIRE. This scene was done roughly with a brush. The hatching with a pen was added later.

WIND, SLEET. The rain on white background was drawn with a pen. On the black it was drawn with a brush in white. On some papers this can be achieved by scratching with a blade or a scalpel.

SURF, FOAM, WIND. This illustration is from a comic book version of Marcus Clarke's *For The Term Of His Natural Life.**

*Peter Foster, Greenhouse, Melbourne, 1986.

EXPLOSIONS can be treated in different ways.

The heavy black blobs suggest the ignition of oil.

The brilliant light from the detonation is reflected in the sea. The uncertain contours of the figures impressionistically suggest flickering light. The curving 'fireworks' show the force.

The lines suggesting the blast must radiate from a single point.

Rough brushstrokes filling in the shadows lend confusion to the scene.

AH! THE POOR HAPLESS CREATURES!

MAY GOD HA MER..

59

LIGHTING of a dramatic nature creates eerie atmospheres.

LIGHTING FROM BELOW. In this case, a desk lamp throws shadows on the forehead and upper cheeks.

LOW LIGHTING inside a tent, with a little back lighting coming from outside.

SIDE LIGHTING from headlights cause a deep shadow down one side of figures.

THE SPOOKY SCENARIO: More can be done by subtle suggestion than by graphically detailed subjects.

MORE SPOOKIES: The spooks themselves can be treated in a variety of ways, limited only by your imagination.

This sequence from 'Ballantyne' shows the supposed 'ghost' of a New Guinea native and the effect it has on the viewers.

Here is the ghost of a pirate appearing while 'live' sailors are right in the middle of a battle.

MORE SPINE TINGLERS

Cowboys, fearing the herd will be spooked by the storm, are themselves spooked.

Gunrunners running scared. What was in the tomb?

Zombies' graveyard hide-out.

A person pretending to be a ghost, uses a sheet and a torch to frighten some natives in New Guinea.

FINALLY: Try to have all your characters show their correct age.

Study shapes.
Don't put a lot of wrinkles on a young face, hoping to achieve the look of old age.

Copy from the art you love best. Your own style will develop as you grow up. That's life in the COMICS business!

Full cheeks; bright eyes.

Big heads; little bodies.

Loose pouches of flesh around the mouth and chin; arthritic knuckles.

Mouth close to nose—no teeth.

FURTHER READING MATTER
Eisner, Will. *Comics and Sequential Art.* Poorhouse Press.

Lee, Stan and Buscema, John. *How to Draw Comics the Marvel Way.* Simon and Schuster.

Ryan, John. *Panel by Panel.* Cassell.

Kemsley, James. *The Cartoon Book.* Ashton Scholastic.

Robinson, Jerry. *The Comics.* Berkley Publishing Corporation.

Herdeg and Pascal. *The Art of the Comic Strip.* The Graphis Press.

Couperie and Horn. *A History of the Comic Strip.* Crown Publishers Inc.

Hogarth, Burne. *Dynamic Anatomy.* Watson-Guptill Publications.